CHANGE THE ATMOSPHERE

With Encouraging Words

Tonya L. Whiteside

THE WHITESIDE GROUP

Rancho Santa Margarita, California

Layout & Cover Design by Written Expressions Concepts & Designs
Photograph of Tonya Whiteside by Earnest Whiteside Photography
Mrs. Whiteside's Stylist- Nicole Hardeman, Backstage Hair Studios

ISBN 978-0-9797393-0-9

The tongue has the power of life and death and those who love it will eat of its fruit.

– Proverbs 18:21 (NLT)

Thinking Positive
Leads to
Speaking Positive.

Speaking Positive
Leads to
Believing Positive.

Believing Positive
Leads to
Living Positive.

FOREWORD

It is with great pleasure and delight that I have been asked to share a few words about this collaborative effort to provide motivational materials presented in this book. Not only is it a honor for me to write this foreword, but an opportunity to express how great it is to have a former track student pass on to others, that which has been passed on to her from various sources and through a multitude of formats. Her sharing with others is truly a gift we both are passionate about and the highest compliment paid to those to whom she believes has motivated her to do so.

As a school administrator, I see firsthand how sharing from time to time words, stories, experiences, and strategies with others has often helped shaped lives, changed the mood of very intense situations, and prompted others to share inspirational and motivational tales. I know for a fact there have been many times I have called upon motivational materials to help guide the outcome of a meeting or move my staff in the direction of the school's goals and objectives. How thankful I am to have shared with others and also been the recipient of other people's experiences made available to me. I am confident this book will serve as a useful resource, as well as, informational and practical for providing the right dose of motivation needed for oneself or when inspiring others.

I applaud Tonya Johnson-Whiteside for writing such an essential book and for including others in her adventure. I look forward to seeing this trend of hers continue and eagerly await other books that will continue in the vein of being a motivation to others.

Bonnie Tolliver, Educational Administrator
Assistant Principal in School District #111,
Kennedy Middle Grade School, Kankakee, Illinois

ACKNOWLEDGEMENTS

Thank you to my husband Earnest, and my two boys Adrien and Andre. I love you more and more every day. I look forward to many more family moments. Special thanks to my parents, Adam and Helen Johnson, and my brother Adam, whose love and support are endless. I thank my mentor and high school track coach Bonnie Tolliver. You believed in me and spoke positive words, even when I wasn't ready to listen. To Aunt Emma (who is 96 years old) and Arlet (recently deceased), thank you for your kind words, wisdom and for calling me your "little warrior." I do not know where I would be if you had not invested in me. I want to also say thanks to all of you who shared your favorite quote or inspirational story with me. It means a lot. Finally, to my church family, extended family and friends, it is because of you that I have been able to change my attitude and lifestyle, and let go of the negative. I no longer want to change my name, just the atmosphere.

INTRODUCTION

Have you ever heard the saying, "sticks and stones may break my bones, but words will never hurt me?" How many of you really believe that? I can tell you from personal experience that words do hurt and the pain lasts a lot longer than sticks and stones. The good news is that we do not have to live our lives by those negative things we have heard or have been told by friends, co-workers or even family members. There are wonderful positive people who believe in you and who are ready to speak positive affirmations into your life. You may know someone (no matter how rough things may seem on the outside) who is always happy. They are always looking at the glass as full and believe in changing the atmosphere. This book is full of those people, who have been sharing motivational stories, inspiring thoughts and positive words that we can live by. In this book, I share those thoughts and words that I am making every effort to add to my daily life.

The next level for you may be just a turn-of-the-page away. Changing the atmosphere will help you and the people you encounter enjoy life. There will always be individuals who are not happy and want you to share in their misery. The quotes in this book are tiny tidbits that can help you make it through the day. It is my desire for you to use this book until you have made each and every quote a part of your atmosphere. There is no deadline for achieving success and you may read a quote today that you may not apply for years to come, which I consider to be the biggest benefit.

I want to encourage you to change your thoughts and words. Changing the atmosphere with positive words can be one of the best things you have ever done. If you are inspired by what you will read, please don't keep it to yourself. Help someone change their atmosphere by your actions and deeds. Be the spark that your friends, family members, acquaintances and co-workers see as someone with a full glass. Enjoy the transformation! Commit to the change and go out and make it a great day!

HOW TO GET THE MOST OUT OF THIS BOOK

You may be a page turner who likes to read a book from cover to cover before digesting the materials. You may be a reader who skips around in a book, until a word or phrase sticks out. You may be someone who wants to get to the point, upon first glance. Regardless of your reading mode, this book will suit your needs.

To get the most from this book, it is helpful if you would follow the "Three S Rule"

1. **See** It (The words on the page)
2. **Say** It (The words from one quote at a time)
3. **Script** It (by writing out the words or even creating a picture)

No matter what technique you use, you can change the atmosphere at work, home and with your friends. Post these positive words in your office, on your desktop and on your bathroom mirror. Share your new positive thinking with everyone you know.

The last step to get the most from this book is to **commit these words to memory**. The good news is that you can repeat this process as often as you desire.

Hold fast to dreams, for if dreams die, life is
a broken-winged bird that cannot fly.
–Langston Hughes

Change your thoughts and
you change your world.
–Norman Vincent Peale

If you want to reach a goal, you must
"see the reaching" in your own mind
before you actually arrive at your goal.
–Zig Ziglar

See it ... Say it ... Script it!

_____

_____

_____

_____

_____

_____

_____

A no today doesn't mean
a no tomorrow.
–Dion Jordan

The time is always right to do what is
right. –Martin Luther King

Build for your team a feeling of oneness,
of dependence upon one another, and of
strength to be derived by unity.
–Vince Lombardi

See it ... Say it ... Script it!

_____

_____

_____

_____

_____

_____

The best thing about the future is that it
comes only one day at a time.
–Abraham Lincoln

Choose a job you love and you will never
have to work a day in your life.
–Confucius

It gives me a deep, comforting sense
that things seen are temporal and
things unseen are eternal.
–Helen Keller

See it ... Say it ... Script it!

_____

_____

_____

_____

_____

_____

The weak can never forgive. Forgiveness
is the attribute of the strong.
–Mahatma Gandhi

Let us never negotiate out of fear,
but let us never fear to negotiate.
–John F. Kennedy

Develop success from failures.
Discouragement and failure are two of
the surest stepping stones to success.
–Dale Carnegie

See it ... Say it ... Script it!

_____

_____

_____

_____

_____

_____

_____

Treat every person that you meet as
if they are the most important
person you have ever met.
–author unknown

We cannot achieve anything of
significance on once a week.
–Marcus Buckingham

If you think you can, you can. And if
you think you can't, you're right.
–Mary Kay Ash

See it ... Say it ... Script it!

_____

_____

_____

_____

_____

_____

If there's a book you really want to read
but it hasn't been written yet, then you
must write it.
–Toni Morrison

Never doubt that a small group of
thoughtful, committed citizens can
change the world. Indeed, it's the only
thing that ever has.
–Margaret Mead

We don't see things as they are we see
them as we are.
–Anais Nin

See it ... Say it ... Script it!

_____

_____

_____

_____

_____

_____

Do what you love and love that
you are doing it.
—author unknown

If you change, then the situation
cannot remain the same.
—Pastor Larry Weaver

Education is power. – Ernest Raheb

Yesterday's tools need to be
sharpened for today.
—Dr. Ralph Tyler

See it ... Say it ... Script it!

_____

_____

_____

_____

_____

_____

We have a stake in one another,
what binds us together is greater
than what drives us apart.
–Barack Obama

You were blessed to bless others. Create
a legacy that will come after you.
–Gwendelyn Boyd

Focus on abundance and
prosperity, not debt.
–Lisa Nichols

See it ... Say it ... Script it!

_____

_____

_____

_____

_____

_____

Prepare to shine. Each day is an
opportunity to live out your life's work.
–Kevin Carroll

Live in the moment, because you will
never get it back. It becomes
just a memory.
–Adam G. Johnson

I know for sure that what we dwell
on is who we become.
–Oprah Winfrey

See it ... Say it ... Script it!

_____

_____

_____

_____

_____

_____

Imagination is more important
than knowledge.
–Albert Einstein

I've learned that you can't have
everything and do everything at the
same time.
–Oprah Winfrey

It is not the strongest of the species that
survives, nor the most intelligent, but
the one most responsive to change.
–Charles Darwin

See it ... Say it ... Script it!

_____

_____

_____

_____

_____

_____

_____

Whatever you fear most has no power.
It is your fear that has the power.
–Oprah Winfrey

Promote yourself, but do
not demote another.
–Israel Salanter

When the character of a man is not clear
to you, look at his friends.
–Japanese Proverb

See it ... Say it ... Script it!

_____

_____

_____

_____

_____

_____

_____

A positive attitude may not solve all
your problems, but it will annoy enough
people to make it worth the effort.
–Herm Albright

I am still determined to be cheerful and
happy, in whatever situation I may be;
for I have also learned from experience
that the greater part of our happiness or
misery depends upon our dispositions,
and not upon our circumstances.
–Martha Washington

See it ... Say it ... Script it!

_____

_____

_____

_____

_____

_____

_____

Believe in yourself! Have faith in your abilities! Without a humble but reasonable confidence in your own powers, you cannot be successful or happy. –Norman Vincent Peale

Great ability develops and reveals itself increasingly with every new assignment. –Baltasar Gracian

A hero is no braver than an ordinary man, but he is braver five minutes longer. –Ralph Waldo Emerson

See it ... Say it ... Script it!

_____

_____

_____

_____

_____

_____

_____

The self is not something ready-made,
but something in continuous formation
through choice of action.
–John Dewey

If you limit your choices to only what
seems possible or reasonable, you
disconnect yourself from what you truly
want, and all that is left is a compromise.
–Robert Fritz

Those who dream by day are cognizant
of many things which escape those who
dream only by night.
–Edgar Allen Poe

See it ... Say it ... Script it!

_____

_____

_____

_____

_____

_____

_____

Many persons have a wrong idea of what
constitutes true happiness. It is not
attained through self-gratification, but
through fidelity to a worthy purpose.
–Helen Keller

One is not necessarily born with
courage, but one is born with potential.
Without courage, we cannot practice
any other virtue with consistency. We
can't be kind, true, merciful,
generous or honest.
–Maya Angelou

See it ... Say it ... Script it!

_____

_____

_____

_____

_____

_____

To inspire loyalty, let others see the
greatness within you, or what it is that
you want them to believe in. You
accomplish this by being the one who
does what is right, even when an easier
course of action is readily available.
–Dr. David J. Lieberman

For everything you have missed, you
have gained something else; and for
everything you gain, you lose something.
–Ralph Waldo Emerson

See it ... Say it ... Script it!

_____

_____

_____

_____

_____

_____

_____

Kind words can be short and easy to speak, but their echoes are truly endless.
—Mother Teresa

Even if you're on the right track, you'll get run over if you just sit there.
—Will Rogers

You can make more friends in two months by becoming interested in other people than you can in two years by trying to get other people interested in you. —Dale Carnegie

See it ... Say it ... Script it!

Let us make one point, that we meet
each other with a smile, when it is
difficult to smile. Smile at each other and
make time for each other in your family.
–Mother Teresa

You may have to fight a battle
more than once to win it.
–Margaret Thatcher

It's so clear that you have
to cherish everyone.
–Alice Walker

See it ... Say it ... Script it!

_____

_____

_____

_____

_____

_____

_____

The gift of love is the greatest. It's a difficult thing because there are people I know that I can't stand. But, love doesn't mean affection. It means treating them justly even when they are terrible people.
–Janet Collins

Drive thy business; let it not drive thee.
–Benjamin Franklin

Avoid putting yourself before others, and you can become a leader among men. –author unknown

See it ... Say it ... Script it!

_____

_____

_____

_____

_____

_____

_____

When dealing with people, let us
remember we are not dealing with
creatures of logic. We are dealing with
creatures of emotion, creatures bustling
with prejudices and motivated
by pride and vanity.
–Dale Carnegie

By conducting a dialogue with our past,
we are searching how to go forward.
–Kiyoko Takeda

Here's to the past. Thank God it's past!
–author unknown

See it ... Say it ... Script it!

_____

_____

_____

_____

_____

_____

_____

You have to be willing
to think the unthinkable.
–Toni Morrison

Ability is nothing without opportunity.
–Napolean

No one can make you feel inferior
without your consent.
–Eleanor Roosevelt

Strong lives are motivated by dynamic
purposes; the most glowing successes are
but reflections of an inner fire.
–Kenneth Hildebrand

See it ... Say it ... Script it!

_____

_____

_____

_____

_____

_____

Communication.
It is not only the essence of being
human, but also a vital property of life.
–John A. Pierce

When your work speaks
for itself, don't interrupt.
–Henry J. Kaiser

Seeing things not for what they are but
for what they might be, creates
opportunity. –Carolyn Kepcher

Keep hope alive! –Jesse Jackson

See it ... Say it ... Script it!

_____

_____

_____

_____

_____

_____

_____

From what we get, we can make a living:
what we give, however, makes a life.
–Arthur Ashe

I really love this business. The bad goes
with it. If it's all good, it's no good.
–Sarah Vaughan

You got to know your opponent. You got
to know their strengths, their weakness,
see how they move...
–Althea Gibson

See it ... Say it ... Script it!

_____

_____

_____

_____

_____

_____

No matter what accomplishment you
achieve, somebody helps you.
–**Althea Gibson**

The price of greatness is responsibility.
–**Sir Winston Churchill**

The best way to have a good idea
is to have lots of ideas.
–**Linus Pauling**

See it ... Say it ... Script it!

_____

_____

_____

_____

_____

_____

Be not afraid of greatness; some are born
great, some achieve greatness, and some
have greatness thrust upon them.
-William Shakespeare

Happiness is not a station you arrive at,
but a manner of traveling.
-author unknown

The only real mistake is the one from
which we learn nothing.
-John Powell

See it ... Say it ... Script it!

_____

_____

_____

_____

_____

_____

Opportunity may knock only once,
but temptation leans on the doorbell.
–author unknown

Our patience will achieve
more than our force.
–Edmund Burke

The secret of getting
ahead is getting started.
–Mark Twain

See it ... Say it ... Script it!

_____

_____

_____

_____

_____

_____

Character cannot be developed in ease
and quiet. Only through experience of
trial and suffering can the soul be
strengthened, ambition inspired and
success achieved.
–Helen Keller

Life does not have to be perfect
to be wonderful.
–Annette Funicello

We aim above the mark to hit the mark.
–Ralph Waldo Emerson

See it ... Say it ... Script it!

_____

_____

_____

_____

_____

_____

Destiny is not a matter of chance;
it is a matter of choice.
–William Jennings Bryan

A life isn't significant except
for its impact on other lives.
–Jackie Robinson

Our lives begin to end the day we
become silent about things that matter.
–Martin Luther King

See it ... Say it ... Script it!

_____

_____

_____

_____

_____

_____

Life is never made unbearable by
circumstances, but only by lack
of meaning and purpose.
–Viktor Frankl

We make a living by what we get,
we make a life by what we give.
–Norman MacFinan

The best way to escape
your problem is to solve it.
–author unknown

See it ... Say it ... Script it!

_____

_____

_____

_____

_____

_____

There are two ways of spreading
light...To be the candle or the mirror
that reflects it.
−Edith Wharton

Somewhere out there is a unique place
for you to help others − a unique life role
for you to fill that only you can fill.
−Thomas Kinkade

The most common way people give up
their power is by thinking
they don't have any.
−Alice Walker

See it ... Say it ... Script it!

Gratitude helps you to grow and expand.
Gratitude brings joy and laughter
into your lives and into the lives
of all those around you.
–Eileen Caddy

If we did all the things we are capable of,
we would literally astound ourselves.
–Thomas Edison

This world belongs to the enthusiastic.
–Ralph Waldo Emerson

See it ... Say it ... Script it!

_____

_____

_____

_____

_____

_____

Every adversity, every failure, and every
heartbreak carries with it the seed of an
equivalent or greater benefit.
–Napolean Hill

One who gains strength by overcoming
obstacles possesses the only strength
which can overcome adversity.
–Albert Schweitzer

Great things are a series of
small things brought together.
–Vincent VanGogh

See it ... Say it ... Script it!

_____

_____

_____

_____

_____

_____

_____

The best way out is always through.
—Robert Frost

Think beyond your lifetime if you want
to accomplish something truly
worthwhile.
—Walt Disney

Failure is impossible.
—Susan B. Anthony

Whatever you are, be a good one.
—Abraham Lincoln

See it ... Say it ... Script it!

_____

_____

_____

_____

_____

_____

_____

You add value to people
when you value them.
–John C. Maxwell

No man can become rich
without himself enriching others.
–Andrew Carnegie

All of you were given two great gifts:
your mind and your time.
–Robert T. Kiyosaki

See it ... Say it ... Script it!

_____

_____

_____

_____

_____

_____

_____

Self-respect is the gateway to
self-esteem. -Dr. David Lieberman

Nobody but Jesus.
-Bishop James D. Carrington

Accept the fact that you'll have to let go
of some emotional baggage. Try seeing
things from a different perspective.
-Bradley Trevor Greive

See it ... Say it ... Script it!

Nothing contributes so much to
tranquilize the mind as a steady
purpose—a point on which the soul may
fix its intellectual eye.
-Mary Shelley

Trust thyself.
-Ralph Waldo Emerson

The truth is, we are all born with
potential greatness, and blessed with
numerous opportunities to soar to
dizzying new heights. -Bradley Trevor Greive

See it ... Say it ... Script it!

_____

_____

_____

_____

_____

_____

We are what we repeatedly do.
Excellence, therefore, is not an act but a
habit. –Aristotle

When faced with a difficult choice to
make, ask yourself: Which one will
make a difference and who will
remember 5 years from now? This
thought often makes the choice far easier
than you think. –Chris Chapel

See it ... Say it ... Script it!

_____

_____

_____

_____

_____

_____

_____

Kindness in words creates confidence;
kindness in thinking creates
profoundness; kindness in feeling
creates love. –Lao Tzu

There is a supply for every demand.
–Florence Scovel Shinn

Life's most persistent and urgent
question is: What are we doing for
others?" There are two ways of
spreading light: to be the candle or the
mirror that reflects it.
–Edith Wharton

See it ... Say it ... Script it!

_____

_____

_____

_____

_____

_____

_____

10% of life is what happens to you,
90% of life is how you react to it.
–Dennis P. Kimbro

Become the change you want
to see in the world.
–Mahatma Ghandi

Keep in mind that whatever you do,
mistakes are part of life. So don't waste
time kicking yourself for the past.
–Bradley Trevor Greive

See it ... Say it ... Script it!

_____

_____

_____

_____

_____

_____

If they don't know that you care, they
won't care what you know.
–author unknown

Art is not a mirror held up to reality, but
a hammer with which to shape it.
–Bertolt Brecht

Wherever you are – be all there.
–Jim Elliot

See it ... Say it ... Script it!

_____

_____

_____

_____

_____

_____

_____

If you are not fired with enthusiasm,
you will be fired with enthusiasm.
-Vince Lombardi

The person interested in success has to
learn to view failure as a healthy,
inevitable part of the process of getting
to the top. **-Joyce Brothers**

Only when we are no longer
afraid do we begin to live.
-Dorothy Thompson

See it ... Say it ... Script it!

_____

_____

_____

_____

_____

_____

_____

Thought is free.
–William Shakespeare

The imagination equips us to perceive reality, when it is not fully materialized.
–Mary Caroline Richards

Give yourself something to work towards constantly.
–Mary Kay Ash

See it ... Say it ... Script it!

_____

_____

_____

_____

_____

_____

_____

It's so hard when I have to,
and so easy when I want to.
–**Sondra Anice Barnes**

Winning isn't everything,
but wanting to win is.
–**Vince Lombardi**

The only way to discover the limits
of the possible, is to go beyond
them and into the impossible.
–**Arthur C. Clarke**

See it ... Say it ... Script it!

_____

_____

_____

_____

_____

_____

_____

In this world you must be oh so smart or oh so pleasant. Well, for years I was smart. I recommend pleasant.
–Elwood P. Dowd from the movie, "Harvey"

When you do what you love, you can pull back the bed sheets every morning feeling excited about beginning another day, and you'll be filled with a heartfelt joy that is highly contagious.
–Bradley Trevor Greive

Play with passion, refuse to lose.
–Coach Joe B. Miller

See it ... Say it ... Script it!

_____

_____

_____

_____

_____

_____

Let nothing dim the light
that shines from within.
–Maya Angelou

A teacher affects eternity; he can never
tell where his influence stops.
–Henry Adams

Discovery consists of looking at the same
thing as everyone else and thinking
something different.
–Roger VonOech

See it ... Say it ... Script it!

_____

_____

_____

_____

_____

_____

If they say you can't, if they say you're
not strong enough, if they say no one has
ever done it before, you always say... Just
watch! –author unknown

There is always someone prepared
to help those who ask.
–Bradley Trevor Greive

Anything that changes your values
changes your behavior.
–George Sheehan

See it ... Say it ... Script it!

_____

_____

_____

_____

_____

_____

_____

Appreciative words are the most
powerful force for good on earth!
–George W. Crane

Leadership is action not position.
–Donald H. McGannon

It is commitment, not authority
that produces results.
–William Gore

See it ... Say it ... Script it!

_____

_____

_____

_____

_____

_____

People tend to resist that which is forced upon them. People tend to support that which they help to create.
                    –Vince Pfaff

Asking for help is not a weakness,
it's a strength.
                    –Martha Manning

Passion persuades.
                    –Anita Roddick

See it ... Say it ... Script it!

_____

_____

_____

_____

_____

_____

_____

Faith is not something to grasp,
it is something to grow into.
–Mahatma Gandhi

A man sees in the world what
he carries in his heart.
–Johann Wolfgang Goethe

Accept challenges so that you may
feel the exhilaration of victory.
–George S. Patton

See it ... Say it ... Script it!

_____

_____

_____

_____

_____

_____

Adventure is worthwhile.
–Amelia Earhart

Life's challenges are not supposed to paralyze you; they're supposed to help you discover who you are.
–Bernice Johnson Reagon

Unless a man undertakes more than he possibly can do, he will never do all that he can.
–Henry Drummond

See it ... Say it ... Script it!

_____

_____

_____

_____

_____

_____

You can gain strength, courage, and confidence by every experience in which you really stop to look fear in the face. You must do the thing which you think you cannot do. –Eleanor Roosevelt

Man shapes himself through decisions that shape his environment. —Rene Dubos

Again and again, the impossible problem is solved when we see that the problem is only a tough decision waiting to be made. –Robert H. Schuller

See it ... Say it ... Script it!

_____

_____

_____

_____

_____

_____

_____

Our lives improve only when we take
chances – and the first and most
difficult risk we can take is to
be honest with ourselves.
–Walter Anderson

Tell me and I forget, show me and I
remember, involve me and I understand.
–author unknown

We should never permit ourselves to do
anything that we are not willing to
see our children do.
–Brigham Young

See it ... Say it ... Script it!

_____

_____

_____

_____

_____

_____

_____

Anyone who has never made a mistake
has never tried anything new.
–**Albert Einstein**

The pessimist sees difficulty in every
opportunity. The optimist sees the
opportunity in every difficulty.
–**Winston Churchill**

Don't ask for a lighter load,
but rather a strong back.
–**author unknown**

See it ... Say it ... Script it!

_____

_____

_____

_____

_____

_____

You learn as much from those who have
failed as from those who have succeeded.
–Michael Johnson

When a man finds no peace within
himself, it is useless to seek it elsewhere.
–L. A. Rouchefolicauld

Real success is finding your lifework
in the work that you love.
–David McCullough

See it ... Say it ... Script it!

_____

_____

_____

_____

_____

_____

Some make it happen, some watch it happen, and some say, "What happened?"
-author unknown

Things turn out best for people who make the best of the way things turn out.
-John Wooden

It is quite possible to work without results, but never will there be results without work.
-author unknown

See it ... Say it ... Script it!

_____

_____

_____

_____

_____

_____

_____

May you live all the days of your life.
–Jonathan Swift

Dreams are renewable. No matter what
our age or condition, there are still
untapped possibilities within us and
new beauty waiting to be born.
–Dr. Dale Turner

I'll take today over yesterday ... any day!
There is hope and encouragement for
tomorrow and the best is yet to come!
–Monica Y. Daugherty

See it ... Say it ... Script it!

_____

_____

_____

_____

_____

_____

_____

Teamwork is only effective when each
member uses their special skills.
-author unknown

Close the gap between what we say
and what we do.
-Gwendelyn Boyd

A true vision is never fulfilled; as soon
as one facet of it becomes realized, it
expresses itself in expanding
opportunities.
-Bobbi DePorter

See it ... Say it ... Script it!

_____

_____

_____

_____

_____

_____

Always do your best at being yourself.
–Mark Sanborn

Trust yourself. Create the kind of
self that you will be happy to live with
all of your life.
–Foster C. McClellan

Be a model of your vision.
Live it so people can see what it is.
–Bobbi DePorter

See it ... Say it ... Script it!

_____

_____

_____

_____

_____

_____

_____

There are no unimportant jobs, just
people who feel unimportant doing their
jobs.
–Mark Sanborn

Excellent organizations are
a hive of champions.
–Tom Peters

Persistence may prove to be rewarding.
–author unknown

See it ... Say it ... Script it!

_____

_____

_____

_____

_____

_____

_____

You are who you choose to be.
–The Iron Giant

Indifference and neglect often do much
more damage than outright dislike.
–J. K. Rowling

You must take your chance.
–William Shakespeare

See it ... Say it ... Script it!

_____

_____

_____

_____

_____

_____

_____

You always pass failure
on the way to success.
–Mickey Rooney

Nobody ever died of laughter.
–Max Beerbohm

The only abnormality is
the incapacity of love.
–Anais Nin

See it ... Say it ... Script it!

It's never too late, in fiction
or in life, to revise.
–Nancy Thayer

Don't be afraid your life will end;
be afraid that it will never begin.
–Grace Hansen

One person with courage makes a
majority. –Andrew Jackson

See it ... Say it ... Script it!

_____

_____

_____

_____

_____

_____

_____

It's not what you call me,
but what I answer to.
–African Proverb

We are what we repeatedly do.
Excellence, therefore, is not an act but a
habit.
–Aristotle

Success is built on relationships.
–Mark Sanborn

See it ... Say it ... Script it!

_____

_____

_____

_____

_____

_____

_____

Don't just stand there, make it happen.
–Lee Iacocca

It's not life's job to make you happy.
It is your job to make life happy.
–Jackson Thomas

You can plant a dream.
–Anne Campbell

See it ... Say it ... Script it!

_____

_____

_____

_____

_____

_____

_____

We accomplish things by directing our
desires, not by ignoring them.
–author unknown

Be an opener of doors...
–Ralph Waldo Emerson

We rise by lifting others.
–Robert Green Ingersoll

See it ... Say it ... Script it!

_____

_____

_____

_____

_____

_____

Vision and mission motivate.
–Andrew Bennett

Love the moment, and the energy of that
moment will spread beyond all
boundaries **–Corita Kent**

A failure is an event, never a person.
–William D. Brown

A smile is an inexpensive
way to improve your looks.
–author unknown

See it ... Say it ... Script it!

So don't get tired of doing what is good.

Don't get discouraged and give up,

for we will reap a harvest of blessings

at the appropriate time.

– Galatians 6:9 (NLT)

ABOUT THE AUTHOR

Tonya L. Whiteside has more than 15 years experience in training and presenting motivational workshops. The Hopkins Park, Illinois native joined the Army Reserves after graduating from high school. She earned a Bachelor of Arts degree in criminal justice from the University of Arkansas at Pine Bluff. Tonya also holds Designated Subjects Credentials in Career Development, Human Service and Law Enforcement Occupations and she currently enrolled in graduate school at Capella University, where she is pursuing a master's degree in human services.

Tonya is known for inspiring young people as an educator and presenter for diversity leaderships programs across the country. She provides community service as an active member of Delta Sigma Theta Sorority, Inc. She shares her angelic voice with the world as a member of the three-time gospel recording group, Brent Jones and the Total Praise (T.P) Mobb.

Tonya is featured in Orange Coast Magazine. The article highlights her love and passion as a mother. Tonya resides in Southern California with three handsome men – her husband, Earnest, and two sons – Adrien and Andre. She is the founder of The Whiteside Group and uses her life experiences, professional education, training and work experience to inspire others.

CONTACT INFORMATION

Tonya L. Whiteside is available for speaking engagements and workshops. For availability and additional information, contact:

Tonya L. Whiteside
The Whiteside Group
31441 Santa Margarita Pkwy., Ste., A #344
Rancho Santa Margarita, CA 92688

Email: tonya@thewhitesidegroup.net

THE WHITESIDE GROUP

www.thewhitesidegroup.net

BOOK ORDER FORM

To order additional copies of **Change the Atmosphere with Encouraging Words**, *mail and make check or money order payable to:*

The Whiteside Group
31441 Santa Margarita Pkwy., Ste., A #344
Rancho Santa Margarita, CA 92688

For additional information, visit www.thewhitesidegroup.net or email: tonya@thewhitesidegroup.net

United States Residents: Include $14.95 plus $3.50 for shipping and handling, per book. California residents must add the applicable county sales tax.

Volume discounts are available. Please contact The Whiteside Group at the address, phone or email address listed above.

NAME: _____

ADDRESS: _____

CITY: _____ STATE _____ ZIP: _____

DAYTIME PHONE: ( ) _____ - _____ Ext. _____

EVENING PHONE: ( ) _____ - _____

QUANTITY: _____ AMOUNT ENCLOSED: $ _____

Amount must be in USD only **Please allow 4 to 6 weeks for your book(s) to arrive. No COD orders.**   09/07

www.ingramcontent.com/pod-product-compliance
Lightning Source LLC
LaVergne TN
LVHW021543080426
835509LV00019B/2813